How Great Thou Art!

How Great Thou Art!

Favorite Religious Verses
Of Faith and Inspiration
Selected by Benjamin Whitley
Illustrated by Don Dubowski

♔

Hallmark Crown Editions

HOW GREAT THOU ART!

HOW GREAT THOU ART!

O Lord my God! When I in awesome wonder
Consider all the worlds Thy hands have made,
I see the stars, I hear the rolling thunder,
Thy pow'r throughout the universe displayed,

Then sings my soul, my Savior God to Thee;
How great Thou art, how great Thou art!
Then sings my soul, my Savior God to Thee;
How great Thou art, how great Thou art!

When through the woods and forest glades I wander
And hear the birds sing sweetly in the trees;
When I look down from lofty mountain grandeur
And hear the brook and feel the gentle breeze;

Then sings my soul, my Savior God to Thee;
How great Thou art, how great Thou art!
Then sings my soul, my Savior God to Thee;
How great Thou art, how great Thou art!

And when I think that God, His Son not sparing,
Sent Him to die, I scarce can take it in;—
That on the cross my burden gladly bearing,
He bled and died to take away my sin;—

Then sings my soul, my Savior God to Thee;
How great Thou art, how great Thou art!
Then sings my soul, my Savior God to Thee;
How great Thou art, how great Thou art!

When Christ shall come with shout of acclamation
And take me home, what joy shall fill my heart!
Then I shall bow in humble adoration
And there proclaim, my God, how great Thou art!

Then sings my soul, my Savior God to Thee;
How great Thou art, how great Thou art!
Then sings my soul, my Savior God to Thee;
How great Thou art, how great Thou art!

CARL BOBERG
Translated by Stuart K. Hine

THE LARGER PRAYER

At first I prayed for Light:
  Could I but see the way,
How gladly, swiftly would I walk
  To everlasting day!

And next I prayed for Strength:
  That I might tread the road
With firm, unfaltering feet, and win
  The heaven's serene abode.

And then I asked for Faith:
  Could I but trust my God,
I'd live enfolded in His peace,
  Though foes were all abroad.

But now I pray for Love:
  Deep love to God and man,
A living love that will not fail,
  However dark His plan.

And Light and Strength and Faith
  Are opening everywhere;
God only waited for me, till
  I prayed the larger prayer.

EDNA D. CHENEY

BARTER

Life has loveliness to sell,
    All beautiful and splendid things,
Blue waves whitened on a cliff,
    Soaring fire that sways and sings,
And children's faces looking up
Holding wonder like a cup.

Life has loveliness to sell,
    Music like a curve of gold,
Scent of pine trees in the rain,
    Eyes that love you, arms that hold,
And for your spirit's still delight,
Holy thoughts that star the night.

Spend all you have for loveliness,
    Buy it and never count the cost;
For one white singing hour of peace
    Count many a year of strife well lost,
And for a breath of ecstasy
Give all you have been, or could be.

SARA TEASDALE

THE PSALM OF LIFE

Tell me not, in mournful numbers,
    Life is but an empty dream!—
For the soul is dead that slumbers,
    And things are not what they seem.

Life is real! Life is earnest!
    And the grave is not its goal;
Dust thou art, to dust returnest,
    Was not spoken of the soul.

Not enjoyment, and not sorrow,
    Is our destined end or way;
But to act, that each tomorrow
    Find us farther than today.

Art is long, and Time is fleeting,
    And our hearts, though stout and brave,
Still, like muffled drums, are beating
    Funeral marches to the grave.

In the world's broad field of battle,
    In the bivouac of life,
Be not like dumb, driven cattle!
    Be a hero in the strife!

Trust no Future, howe'er pleasant!
  Let the dead Past bury its dead!
Act, act in the living Present!
  Heart within, and God o'erhead!

Lives of great men all remind us
  We can make our lives sublime,
And, departing, leave behind us
  Footprints on the sands of time.

Footprints, that perhaps another,
  Sailing o'er life's solemn main,
A forlorn and shipwrecked brother,
  Seeing, shall take heart again.

Let us then be up and doing,
  With a heart for any fate;
Still achieving, still pursuing,
  Learn to labor and to wait.

                    HENRY WADSWORTH LONGFELLOW

OUT IN THE FIELDS WITH GOD

The little cares that fretted me
   I lost them yesterday,
Among the fields above the sea,
   Among the winds at play,
Among the lowing of the herds,
   The rustling of the trees,
Among the singing of the birds,
   The humming of the bees.

The foolish fears of what might pass,
   I cast them all away
Among the clover-scented grass,
   Among the new-mown hay,
Among the husking of the corn,
   Where drowsy poppies nod
Where ill thoughts die and good are born—
   Out in the fields with God.

AUTHOR UNKNOWN

BATTLE HYMN OF THE REPUBLIC

Mine eyes have seen the glory
   of the coming of the Lord;
He is trampling out the vintage
   where the grapes of wrath are stored;
He hath loosed the fateful lightning
   of His terrible swift sword;
His truth is marching on.

Glory! glory, hallelujah!
Glory! glory, hallelujah!
His truth is marching on.

I have seen Him in the watchfires
   of a hundred circling camps;
They have builded Him an altar
   in the evening dews and damps;
I can read His righteous sentence
   by the dim and flaring lamps;
His day is marching on.

Glory! glory, hallelujah!
Glory! glory, hallelujah!
His day is marching on.

He has sounded forth the trumpet
    that shall never sound retreat;
He is sifting out the hearts of men
    before His judgment seat.
O be swift, my soul, to answer Him!
    be jubilant, my feet!
Our God is marching on.

Glory! glory, hallelujah!
Glory! glory, hallelujah!
Our God is marching on.

In the beauty of the lilies
    Christ was born across the sea,
With a glory in His bosom
    that transfigures you and me;
As He died to make men holy,
    let us die to make men free;
While God is marching on.

Glory! glory, hallelujah!
Glory! glory, hallelujah!
While God is marching on.

JULIA WARD HOWE

STILL, STILL WITH THEE

Still, still with Thee, when purple morning breaketh,
When the bird waketh, and the shadows flee;
Fairer than morning, lovelier than the daylight,
Dawns the sweet consciousness. I am with Thee.

Alone with Thee, amid the mystic shadows,
The solemn hush of nature newly born;
Alone with Thee in breathless adoration,
In the calm dew and freshness of the morn.

When sinks the soul, subdued by toil, to slumber,
Its closing eyes look up to Thee in prayer;
Sweet the repose beneath Thy wings o'ershading,
But sweeter still to wake and find Thee there.

So shall it be at last, in that bright morning
When the soul waketh, and life's shadows flee;
Oh, in that hour, fairer than daylight dawning,
Shall rise the glorious thought—I am with Thee. Amen.

HARRIET BEECHER STOWE

AMAZING GRACE

Amazing grace! how sweet the sound,
That saved a wretch like me!
I once was lost, but now am found,
Was blind, but now I see.

'Twas grace that taught my heart to fear,
And grace my fears relieved;
How precious did that grace appear
The hour I first believed!

Thro' many dangers, toils and snares,
I have already come;
'Tis grace hath bro't me safe thus far
And grace will lead me home.

When we've been there ten thousand years,
Bright shining as the sun,
We've no less days to sing God's praise
Than when we first begun.

JOHN NEWTON

TODAY

So here hath been dawning
  Another blue day:
Think, wilt thou let it
  Slip useless away?

Out of Eternity
  This new day is born;
Into Eternity
  At night will return.

Behold it afore time,
  No eye ever did:
So soon it forever
  From all eyes is hid.

Here hath been dawning
  Another blue day:
Think, wilt thou let it
  Slip useless away?

THOMAS CARLYLE

GOOD-BYE

Good-bye, proud world! I'm going home:
Thou art not my friend, and I'm not thine.
Long through thy weary crowds I roam;
A river-ark on the ocean brine,
Long I've been tossed like the driven foam;
But now, proud world! I'm going home.

Good-bye to Flattery's fawning face;
To Grandeur with his wise grimace;
To upstart Wealth's averted eye;
To supple Office, low and high;
To crowded halls, to court and street;
To frozen hearts and hasting feet;
To those who go and those who come;
Good-bye, proud world! I'm going home.

I am going to my own hearth-stone,
Bosomed in yon green hills alone,—
A secret nook in a pleasant land,
Whose groves the frolic fairies planned;
Where arches green, the livelong day,
Echo the blackbird's roundelay,
And vulgar feet have never trod
A spot that is sacred to thought and God.

Oh, when I am safe in my sylvan home,
I tread on the pride of Greece and Rome;
And when I am stretched beneath the pines,
Where the evening star so holy shines,
I laugh at the lore and the pride of man,
At the sophist schools and the learned clan;
For what are they all in their high conceit,
When man in the bush with God may meet?

RALPH WALDO EMERSON

I SHALL NOT
PASS THIS WAY AGAIN

I shall not pass this way again —
   Although it bordered be with flowers,
   Although I rest in fragrant bowers,
     And hear the singing
     Of song-birds winging
To highest heaven their gladsome flight;
Though moons are full and stars are bright,
And winds and waves are softly sighing,
While leafy trees make low replying;
Though voices clear in joyous strain
Repeat a jubilant refrain;
Though rising suns their radiance throw
On summer's green and winter's snow,
In such rare splendor that my heart
Would ache from scenes like these to part;
     Though beauties heighten,
     And life-lights brighten,
And joys proceed from every pain, —
I shall not pass this way again.

Then let me pluck the flowers that blow,
And let me listen as I go

To music rare
That fills the air;
And let hereafter
Songs and laughter
Fill every pause along the way;
And to my spirit let me say:
"O soul, be happy; soon 'tis trod,
The path made thus for thee by God.
Be happy, thou, and bless His name
By whom such marvellous beauty came."
And let no chance by me be lost
To kindness show at any cost.
I shall not pass this way again;
Then let me now relieve some pain,
Remove some barrier from the road,
Or lighten some one's heavy load;
A helping hand to this one lend,
Then turn some other to befriend.

O God, forgive
That now I live
As if I might, sometime, return
To bless the weary ones that yearn

For help and comfort every day,—
For there be such along the way.
O God, forgive that I have seen
The beauty only, have not been
Awake to sorrow such as this;
That I have drunk the cup of bliss
Remembering not that those there be
Who drink the dregs of misery.

I love the beauty of the scene,
Would roam again o'er fields so green;
But since I may not, let me spend
My strength for others to the end,—
For those who tread on rock and stone,
And bear their burdens all alone,
Who loiter not in leafy bowers,
Nor hear the birds nor pluck the flowers.
A larger kindness give to me,
A deeper love and sympathy;
        Then, O, one day
        May someone say—
Remembering a lessened pain—
"Would she could pass this way again."

                                    EVA ROSE YORK

A MIGHTY FORTRESS IS OUR GOD

A mighty fortress is our God,
  a bulwark never failing;
Our helper He, amid the flood
  of mortal ills prevailing.
For still our ancient foe
  doth seek to work us woe;
His craft and pow'r are great,
  and, armed with cruel hate,
On earth is not his equal.

That word above all earthly pow'rs
  no thanks to them abith:
The Spirit and the gifts are ours
  thro' Him who with us sideth.
Let goods and kindred go,
  this mortal life also;
The body they may kill:
  God's truth abideth still,
His kingdom is forever.

MARTIN LUTHER

GOD IS LOVE

God is love; His mercy brightens
   All the path in which we rove;
Bliss He wakes and woe He lightens:
   God is wisdom, God is love.

Chance and change are busy ever;
   Man decays and ages move;
But His mercy waneth never:
   God is wisdom, God is love.

Even the hour that darkest seemeth
   Will His changeless goodness prove;
From the mist His brightness streameth:
   God is wisdom, God is love.

He with earthly cares entwineth
   Hope and comfort from above:
Everywhere His glory shineth:
   God is wisdom, God is love.

JOHN BOWRING

THE LAMP OF LIFE

Always we are following a light,
Always the light recedes; with groping hands
We stretch toward this glory, while the lands
We journey through are hidden from our sight
Dim and mysterious, folded deep in night,
We care not, all our utmost need demands
Is but the light, the light! So still it stands
Surely our own if we exert our might.
Fool! Never can'st thou grasp this fleeting gleam,
Its glowing flame would die if it were caught,
Its value is that it doth always seem
But just a little farther on. Distraught,
But lighted ever onward, we are brought
Upon our way unknowing, in a dream.

AMY LOWELL

FOR THY LOVE'S IMMENSITY

For the firefly's twinkling light,
For the precious gift of sight,
For the lilac scented night,
    Father of all, accept our thanks!

For the quiet of the dawn,
For the dappled, soft-eyed fawn,
For the toy-strewn, trampled lawn,
    Father of all, accept our thanks!

For the fern lined forest aisles,
For the bird song that beguiles,
For the kindredship of smiles,
    Father of all, accept our thanks!

For the golden honey-bee,
For the right to disagree,
For Thy love's immensity,
    Father of all, accept our thanks!

EMILY CAREY ALLEMAN

ROCK OF AGES

Rock of Ages, cleft for me,
Let me hide myself in Thee;
Let the water and the blood,
From Thy riven side which flowed,
Be of sin the double cure,
Save me from its guilt and pow'r.

Not the labors of my hands
Can fulfill Thy law's demands;
Could my zeal no respite know,
Could my tears forever flow,
All for sin could not atone;
Thou must save, and Thou alone.

Nothing in my hand I bring,
Simply to Thy cross I cling;
Naked, come to Thee for dress;
Helpless, look to Thee for grace;
Foul, I to the fountain fly,
Wash me, Savior, or I die!

While I draw this fleeting breath,
When mine eyes shall close in death,
When I soar to worlds unknown,
See Thee on Thy judgment throne,
Rock of Ages, cleft for me,
Let me hide myself in Thee.

AUGUSTUS M. TOPLADY

IF I CAN STOP
ONE HEART FROM BREAKING

If I can stop one heart from breaking,
I shall not live in vain;
If I can ease one life the aching,
Or cool one pain,
Or help one fainting robin
Unto his nest again,
I shall not live in vain.

EMILY DICKINSON

TREES

I think that I shall never see
A poem lovely as a tree.

A tree whose hungry mouth is pressed
Against the earth's sweet-flowing breast;

A tree that looks at God all day,
And lifts her leafy arms to pray;

A tree that may in summer wear
A nest of robins in her hair;

Upon whose bosom snow has lain;
Who intimately lives with rain.

Poems are made by fools like me,
But only God can make a tree.

JOYCE KILMER

NEARER, MY GOD, TO THEE

Nearer, my God, to Thee,
  Nearer to Thee!
E'en though it be a cross
  That raiseth me;
Still all my song shall be,
Nearer, my God, to Thee,
  Nearer to Thee!

Though like the wanderer,
  The sun gone down,
Darkness be over me,
  My rest a stone;
Yet in my dreams I'd be
Nearer, my God, to Thee,
  Nearer to Thee!

There let my way appear
  Steps unto heaven;
All that Thou sendest me
  In mercy given;
Angels to beckon me
Nearer, my God, to Thee,
  Nearer to Thee!

Then, with my waking thoughts
   Bright with Thy praise,
Out of my stony griefs,
   Bethel I'll raise;
So by my woes to be
Nearer, my God, to Thee,
   Nearer to Thee!

Or, if on joyful wing,
   Cleaving the sky,
Sun, moon, and stars forgot,
   Upward I fly,
Still all my song shall be
Nearer, my God, to Thee,
   Nearer to Thee!

SARAH FLOWER ADAMS

DON'T TROUBLE TROUBLE

Don't you trouble trouble till trouble troubles you.
Don't you look for trouble; let trouble look for you.
Who feareth hath forsaken the heavenly Father's side;
What He hath undertaken He surely will provide.

The very birds reprove thee with their happy song;
The very flowers teach thee that fretting is a wrong.
"Cheer up," the sparrow chirpeth; "Thy Father feedeth me;
Think how much He careth, oh, lonely child, for thee."

"Fear not," the flowers whisper; "since thus He hath arrayed
The buttercup and daisy, how canst thou be afraid?"
Then don't you trouble trouble till trouble troubles you;
You'll only double trouble, and trouble others too.

MARK GUY PEARSE

[37]

THE OLD RUGGED CROSS

On a hill far away stood an old rugged cross,
The emblem of suff'ring and shame;
And I love that old cross where the dearest and best
For a world of lost sinners was slain.

So I'll cherish the old rugged cross,
Till my trophies at last I lay down;
I will cling to the old rugged cross,
And exchange it some day for a crown.

Oh, that old rugged cross so despised by the world,
Has a wondrous attraction for me;
For the dear Lamb of God left His glory above,
To bear it to dark Calvary.

So I'll cherish the old rugged cross,
Till my trophies at last I lay down;
I will cling to the old rugged cross,
And exchange it some day for a crown.

In the old rugged cross, stained with blood so divine,
A wondrous beauty I see;
For 'twas on that old cross Jesus suffered and died,
To pardon and sanctify me.

So I'll cherish the old rugged cross,
Till my trophies at last I lay down;
I will cling to the old rugged cross,
And exchange it some day for a crown.

To the old rugged cross I will ever be true,
Its shame and reproach gladly bear;
Then He'll call me some day to my home far away,
Where His glory forever I'll share.

So I'll cherish the old rugged cross,
Till my trophies at last I lay down;
I will cling to the old rugged cross,
And exchange it some day for a crown.

GEORGE BENNARD

ALL THINGS BRIGHT
AND BEAUTIFUL

All things bright and beautiful,
    All creatures great and small,
All things wise and wonderful,
    The Lord God made them all.

Each little flower that opens,
    Each little bird that sings,
He made their glowing colours,
    He made their tiny wings.

The purple-headed mountain,
    The river running by,
The sunset, and the morning
    That brightens up the sky,

The cold wind in the winter,
    The pleasant summer sun,
The ripe fruits in the garden,
    He made them every one.

The tall trees in the greenwood,
    The meadows where we play,
The rushes by the water,
    We gather every day.

He gave us eyes to see them,
    And lips that we might tell
How great is God Almighty,
    Who has made all things well.

CECIL FRANCES ALEXANDER

THE LOST CHORD

Seated one day at the Organ,
   I was weary and ill at ease,
And my fingers wandered idly
   Over the noisy keys.

I know not what I was playing,
   Or what I was dreaming then;
But I struck one chord of music,
   Like the sound of a great Amen.

It flooded the crimson twilight,
   Like the close of an angel's Psalm,
And it lay on my fevered spirit
   With a touch of infinite calm.

It quieted pain and sorrow,
   Like love overcoming strife;
It seemed the harmonious echo
   From our discordant life.

It linked all perplexed meanings
    Into one perfect peace,
And trembled away into silence
    As if it were loth to cease.

I have sought but I seek it vainly,
    That one lost chord divine,
Which came from the soul of the Organ
    And entered into mine.

It may be that Death's bright angel
    Will speak in that chord again—
It may be that only in Heaven
    I shall hear that great Amen.

ADELAIDE ANNE PROCTOR

THE LAMB

Little lamb, who made thee?
Dost thou know who made thee?
Gave thee life and bade thee feed
By the stream and o'er the mead;
Gave thee clothing of delight,
Softest clothing, woolly, bright;
Gave thee such a tender voice,
Making all the vales rejoice?
Little lamb, who made thee?
Dost thou know who made thee?

Little lamb, I'll tell thee;
Little lamb, I'll tell thee;
He is called by thy name,
For he calls himself a lamb.
He is meek and he is mild,
He became a little child, —
I a child and thou a lamb,
We are called by his name.
Little lamb, God bless thee!
Little lamb, God bless thee!

WILLIAM BLAKE

HOLY, HOLY, HOLY

Holy, Holy, Holy, Lord God Almighty!
Early in the morning our song shall rise to Thee;
Holy, Holy, Holy! Merciful and Mighty!
God in Three Persons, blessed Trinity!

Holy, Holy, Holy! All the saints adore Thee,
Casting down their golden crowns around the glassy sea;
Cherubim and seraphim falling down before Thee,
Which wert, and art, and evermore shalt be.

Holy, Holy, Holy! Tho' the darkness hide Thee,
Tho' the eye of sinful man Thy glory may not see,
Only Thou art holy; there is none beside Thee
Perfect in pow'r, in love, and purity.

Holy, Holy, Holy, Lord God Almighty!
All Thy works shall praise Thy name,
    in earth, and sky, and sea;
Holy, Holy, Holy! Merciful and Mighty!
God in Three Persons, blessed Trinity!

REGINALD HEBER

THE LORD'S PRAYER

Our Father which art in heaven,
Hallowed be thy name.
Thy kingdom come.
Thy will be done
    in earth, as it is in heaven.

Give us this day
    our daily bread.
And forgive us our debts,
    as we forgive our debtors.
And lead us not into temptation,
    but deliver us from evil:

For thine is the kingdom,
    and the power,
    and the glory,
    forever. Amen.

MATTHEW 6:9-13

PROVIDENCE

Light Shining Out of Darkness

God moves in a mysterious way
    His wonders to perform;
He plants his footsteps in the sea,
    And rides upon the storm.

Deep in unfathomable mines
    Of never-failing skill
He treasures up his bright designs,
    And works his sovereign will.

Ye fearful saints, fresh courage take,
    The clouds ye so much dread
Are big with mercy, and shall break
    In blessings on your head.

Judge not the Lord by feeble sense,
    But trust him for his grace:
Behind a frowning providence
    He hides a smiling face.

His purposes will ripen fast,
    Unfolding every hour;
The bud may have a bitter taste
    But sweet will be the flower.

Blind unbelief is sure to err,
    And scan his work in vain;
God is his own interpreter
    And he will make it plain.

WILLIAM COWPER

HARK!
THE HERALD ANGELS SING

Hark! the herald angels sing,
"Glory to the newborn King;
Peace on earth, and mercy mild;
God and sinners reconciled."
Joyful, all ye nations, rise,
Join the triumph of the skies;
With angelic hosts proclaim,
"Christ is born in Bethlehem."
Hark! the herald angels sing,
"Glory to the newborn King!"

Christ, by highest Heav'n adored,
Christ, the everlasting Lord:
Late in time behold Him come,
Offspring of a virgin's womb.
Veiled in flesh the Godhead see,
Hail th'incarnate Deity!
Pleased as man with men to appear,
Jesus our Immanuel here.
Hark! the herald angels sing,
"Glory to the newborn King!"

CHARLES WESLEY

I NEVER KNEW
A NIGHT SO BLACK

I never knew a night so black
Light failed to follow on its track.
I never knew a storm so gray
It failed to have its clearing day.
I never knew such bleak despair
That there was not a rift, somewhere.
I never knew an hour so drear
Love could not fill it full of cheer!

JOHN KENDRICK BANGS

AN EVENING PRAYER

Now I lay me down to sleep,
I pray Thee, Lord, Thy child to keep;
Thy love go with me all the night
And wake me with the morning light.

AUTHOR UNKNOWN

from CONTEMPLATIONS

When I behold the heavens as in their prime,
   And then the earth, though old, still clad in green,
The stones and trees insensible of time,
   Nor age nor wrinkle on their front are seen;
If winter come, and greenness then do fade,
A spring returns, and they more youthful made;
But man grows old, lies down,
   remains where once he's laid.

By birth more noble than those creatures all,
   Yet seems by nature and by custom cursed—
No sooner born but grief and care makes fall
   That state obliterate he had at first;
Nor youth, nor strength, nor wisdom spring again,
Nor habitations long their names retain,
But in oblivion to the final day remain.

Shall I then praise the heavens, the trees, the earth,
   Because their beauty and their strength last longer?
Shall I wish therefor never to had birth,
   Because they're bigger and their bodies stronger?
Nay, they shall darken, perish, fade, and die,
And when unmade so ever shall they lie;
But man was made for endless immortality.

ANNE BRADSTREET

ST. FRANCIS' PRAYER

Lord, make me an instrument of Thy peace.
Where there is hate, may I bring love;
Where offense, may I bring pardon;
May I bring union in place of discord;
Truth, replacing error;
Faith, where once there was doubt;
Hope, for despair;
Light, where was darkness;
Joy to replace sadness.
Make me not to so crave to be loved as to love.
Help me to learn that in giving I may receive;
In forgetting self, I may find life eternal.

ST. FRANCIS OF ASSISI

THE WINDS OF FATE

One ship drives east and another drives west
  With the selfsame winds that blow.
    'Tis the set of the sails
    And not the gales
Which tells us the way to go.

Like the winds of the sea are the ways of fate,
  As we voyage along through life:
    'Tis the set of the soul
    That decides its goal,
  And not the calm or the strife.

ELLA WHEELER WILCOX

from A STRIP OF BLUE

I do not own an inch of land,
    But all I see is mine, —
The orchard and the mowing-fields,
    The lawns and gardens fine.
The winds my tax-collectors are,
    They bring me tithes divine, —
Wild scents and subtle essences,
    A tribute rare and free;
And, more magnificent than all,
    My window keeps for me
A glimpse of blue immensity, —
    A little strip of sea.

Here sit I, as a little child;
    The threshold of God's door
Is that clear band of chrysoprase
    Now the vast temple floor,
The blinding glory of the dome
    I bow my head before.
Thy universe, O God, is home,
    In height or depth, to me;
Yet here upon thy footstool green
    Content am I to be;
Glad when is oped unto my need
    Some sea-like glimpse of Thee.

                            LUCY LARCOM

IN HEAVENLY LOVE ABIDING

In heavenly love abiding,
No change my heart shall fear;
And safe is such confiding,
For nothing changes here.
The storm may roar without me,
My heart may low be laid;
But God is round about me,
And can I be dismayed?

Wherever He may guide me,
No want shall turn me back;
My Shepherd is beside me,
And nothing can I lack.
His wisdom ever waketh,
His sight is never dim;
He knows the way He taketh,
And I will walk with Him.

Green pastures are before me,
Which yet I have not seen;
Bright skies will soon be o'er me,
Where darkest clouds have been.

My hope I cannot measure,
My path to life is free;
My Saviour has my treasure,
And He will walk with me.

ANNA L. WARING

SONG

The year's at the spring
And day's at the morn;
Morning's at seven:
The hillside's dew-pearled;
The lark's on the wing;
The snail's on the thorn;
God's in his heaven—
All's right with the world!

ROBERT BROWNING
from "Pippa Passes"

WHAT GOD
HATH PROMISED

God hath not promised
Skies always blue,
Flower-strewn pathways
All our lives through;
God hath not promised
Sun without rain,
Joy without sorrow,
Peace without pain.

But God hath promised
Strength for the day,
Rest for the labor,
Light for the way,
Grace for the trials,
Help from above,
Unfailing sympathy,
Undying love.

ANNIE JOHNSON FLINT

BENEATH THE CROSS

Beneath the Cross of Jesus,
    I fain would take my stand,
The shadow of a mighty rock
    Within a weary land;
A home within the wilderness,
    A rest upon the way,
From the burning of the noontide heat,
    And the burden of the day.

Upon the Cross of Jesus,
    Mine eye at times can see
The very dying form of One
    Who suffered there for me.
And from my smitten heart, with tears,
    Two wonders I confess, —
The wonder of His glorious love,
    And my own worthlessness.

I take, O Cross, thy shadow
    For my abiding-place;
I ask no other sunshine than
    The sunshine of His face:

Content to let the world go by.
  To know no gain nor loss,
My sinful self my only shame,
  My glory all, the Cross.

ELIZABETH CECILIA CLEPHANE

from THE CRY OF THE HUMAN

"There is no God," the foolish saith,
  But none "There is no sorrow,"
And nature oft the cry of faith
  In bitter need will borrow:
Eyes, which the preacher could not school,
  By wayside graves are raised,
And lips say, "God be pitiful,"
  Who ne'er said, "God be prais'd."

ELIZABETH BARRETT BROWNING

A THING OF BEAUTY

A thing of beauty is a joy for ever:
Its loveliness increases; it will never
Pass into nothingness; but still will keep
A bower quiet for us, and a sleep
Full of sweet dreams, and health, and quiet breathing.
Therefore, on every morrow, are we wreathing
A flowery band to bind us to the earth,
Spite of despondence, of the inhuman dearth
Of noble natures, of the gloomy days,
Of all the unhealthy and o'er-darkened ways
Made for our searching: yes, in spite of all,
Some shape of beauty moves away the pall
From our dark spirits. Such the sun, the moon,
Trees old and young, sprouting a shady boon
For simple sheep; and such are daffodils
With the green world they live in; and clear rills
That for themselves a cooling covert make
'Gainst the hot season; the mid-forest brake,
Rich with a sprinkling of fair musk-rose blooms:
And such too is the grandeur of the dooms
We have imagined for the mighty dead;
All lovely tales that we have heard or read:
An endless fountain of immortal drink,
Pouring unto us from the heaven's brink.

JOHN KEATS
from *Endymion*

TAKE MY LIFE

Take my life, and let it be
Consecrated, Lord, to Thee.
Take my moments and my days;
Let them flow in ceaseless praise.
Take my hands, and let them move
At the impulse of Thy love.
Take my feet, and let them be
Swift and beautiful for Thee.

Take my voice, and let me sing,
Always, only, for my King.
Take my lips, and let them be
Filled with messages from Thee.
Take my silver and my gold;
Not a mite would I withhold.
Take my intellect, and use
Every power as Thou shalt choose.

Take my will, and make it Thine;
It shall be no longer mine.
Take my heart, it is Thine own;
It shall be Thy royal throne.

Take my love; my Lord, I pour
At Thy feet its treasure-store.
Take myself, and I will be
Ever, only, all for Thee.

FRANCES RIDLEY HAVERGAL

LITTLE THINGS

Little drops of water,
    Little grains of sand
Make the mighty ocean
    And the pleasant land.

Thus the little minutes,
    Humble though they be,
Make the mighty ages
    Of eternity.

JULIA FLETCHER CARNEY

INDEX OF TITLES

Set in Diotima, a rarely used calligraphic
Roman designed for the Stempel foundry
in 1954 by Gudrun Zapf von Hesse.
Printed on Hallmark Buff Vellux paper.
Designed by Joel D. Ravitch.